Celebrations

by F. Isabel Campoy
illustrated by Keunhee Lee

Harcourt

Orlando   Boston   Dallas   Chicago   San Diego

Visit *The Learning Site!*

www.harcourtschool.com

In every month of the year there is something to celebrate. Sometimes, we celebrate a new season. Sometimes, we celebrate a special day.

Some special days help us remember an important event. Others help us remember a person who has done something important.

January

January 1 is New Year's Day. It is the first day of the year. In January, we celebrate the birthday of Martin Luther King, Jr. He was a leader in making things fair for all people.

February

February 14 is Valentine's Day. On this day we give cards, candy, and flowers to the people we love. Some people like to wear something red or pink.

March

March 17 is St. Patrick's Day. On this day people wear green and march in parades. The Irish people brought this celebration to the United States.

April

In April, some people celebrate the beginning of spring. Flowers start to bloom, and baby animals are born. Everything seems fresh and new.

May

May 5 is Cinco de Mayo. On this day, we celebrate Mexican independence. We also celebrate Mother's Day in May. This is the day to tell your mother you love her very much.

June

When June comes, summer is here. School is over and the weather is warm. The days are long, so there is more time to play outside! We also celebrate Father's Day in June. Fathers are special people.

July

July 4 is Independence Day. This is the day we celebrate America's independence from England. People have picnics and march in parades. At night there are fireworks.

August

August is the last month of summer. It is often the hottest month of the year. My family and I go on vacation in August. I celebrate my birthday on August 13!

September

In September, fall is here. The air outside is cooler. In some places, the leaves on the trees change from green to yellow, orange, and red.

12

October

In October we enjoy cooler weather. We watch the leaves start to fall from the trees. October is a time of fall harvests.

November

On the fourth Thursday of November, we celebrate Thanksgiving. We think about what we are thankful for. Then we eat dinner with our family and friends. My favorite Thanksgiving foods are turkey with stuffing and pumpkin pie.

December

In December, winter begins again. If we live where winters are cold, we wear coats, hats, and gloves. We celebrate the holiday season.

On December 31, the year ends and we wait to welcome another new year. Then we can celebrate everything all over again!